THE LONG DISTANCE LOVE GUIDE

THE LONG DISTANCE LOVE GUIDE

CARMEN WILDE

CONTENTS

Introduction	1
1 Understanding Long-Distance Relationships	5
2 Communication Strategies	9
3 Building Trust and Security	13
4 Maintaining Intimacy	17
5 Managing Time Zones and Schedules	21
6 Coping with Stress and Loneliness	25
7 Balancing Personal and Relationship Needs	29
8 Cultural and Interpersonal Differences in Long-Dis	33
9 Support Systems and Community Resources	37
10 Celebrating Milestones and Special Occasions	41
11 Planning Visits and Reunions	45
12 Dealing with Transitions and Uncertainties	49
13 Self-Care and Personal Growth in Long-Distance Rel	53
14 The Future of Your Relationship: Setting Goals and	57
15 Case Studies and Success Stories	61
Conclusion and Final Tips	64

Copyright © 2025 by Carmen Wilde
All rights reserved. No part of this book may be reproduced in any manner whatsoever without written permission except in the case of brief quotations embodied in critical articles and reviews.
First Printing, 2025

Introduction

Keeping the spark alive in a relationship is challenging, but it becomes even more daunting when distance separates you from your loved one. Physical separation can be due to various reasons—be it work commitments, studies, or other personal circumstances. Regardless of what keeps you and your better half apart, having a solid plan is essential to overcoming the hurdles that come with long-distance relationships.

Forethought and meticulous effort in maintaining your relationship **now** can save you a lot of trouble later. By addressing potential issues early on and sealing any cracks in your love ship, you can navigate through tough times with ease.

In an ideal world, your main concern would be how to cherish and celebrate the privilege of being with someone who loves you. Unfortunately, life has a knack for throwing curveballs our way, which can derail even the most promising relationships. Staying connected with a long-distance partner requires **time, effort, and dedication**. Additionally, incorporating stress-relief strategies into your routine can significantly impact your relationship's well-being.

This guide aims to provide invaluable advice and **four key stress-reducing strategies** for long-distance relationships: **communication, planning, predicting, and mindfulness**. These strategies will help you and your partner gain a clear understanding of your relationship, prioritize what matters most, and reduce overall relationship stress.

Expanded Purpose and Scope of the Guide

The **Long Distance Love Guide** is designed to offer practical advice and insights to help couples navigate the complexities of long-distance relationships. Whether your separation is temporary, lasting a few weeks, or prolonged, extending to a year or more, long-distance relationships can thrive and become stress-free with the right approach.

This guide caters to all readers but might be most beneficial for young people, particularly those in college or still living with their parents. It covers various aspects of long-distance relationships, each detailed in its own section. Key topics include transitioning from a physical relationship to a long-distance one, establishing ground rules, maintaining a strong emotional connection, emphasizing the importance of interaction and communication, and offering creative ideas for virtual dates and get-togethers.

Additionally, the guide may include information on special aspects of long-distance relationships that may not apply to everyone, such as those involving children. Lastly, it will provide resources for further assistance and support, ensuring you have all the tools needed to thrive in your long-distance relationship. I hope you find this guide as helpful and insightful as I intend it to be.

Expanded Importance of Maintaining Strong Long-Distance Relationships

In our increasingly globalized world, maintaining an intimate relationship over long distances is becoming more common and can be viewed as a modern rite of passage. Statistics indicate that between 15% and 33% of internet users are involved in long-distance relationships. The rise in international dating services highlights the growing need for guidance in this area.

Despite the increasing prevalence of long-distance relationships, the literature on this topic leaves many questions unanswered. For instance, what are the essential elements of maintaining a strong, computer-mediated romantic relationship? What benefits and challenges accompany such relationships? How do they impact the individuals involved?

The scarcity of comprehensive research on long-distance relationships might suggest that these relationships are too unconventional to warrant serious consideration. However, this perspective is disputable, given the number of people who would benefit from practical advice and guidance. While some cultures still favor face-to-face interactions and remain skeptical of long-distance relationships, these connections are becoming more widespread.

As a result, there is a pressing need for effective guidelines to help individuals navigate their long-distance relationships. This guide serves to fill that gap by offering thoughtful and actionable advice to support couples in maintaining strong, healthy, and fulfilling relationships despite the distance.

CHAPTER 1

Understanding Long-Distance Relationships

Creating and maintaining a long-distance relationship can be an intimidating prospect. The sudden realization of being miles apart can cause a wave of panic. However, there are silver linings to be found. For instance, it allows more personal time, less pressure to always look or act perfect, and freedom to plan cozy nights in with your favorite PJs, a great movie, and a bottle of wine. Long-distance relationships may not be for everyone, but with the right mindset and effort, they can work beautifully.

Author Atra Eimelya, well-versed in the realm of long-distance relationships, highlights how the internet has made it easier to connect across great distances in less time. Before the digital age, passionate love letters and prolonged courtship were the norms. While the medium has changed, the essence of loyalty and trust remains crucial. Modern technology ensures we no longer wait days or weeks for communication, with messages exchanged instantly. This convenience helps mitigate misunderstandings and fosters continuous connection—essential for overcoming the inevitable time and effort needed.

For many couples, geographical separation stems from personal or professional commitments, such as work relocations or military assignments. Emotional stress can be particularly taxing when one partner is frequently away. If both partners are in the same country, visits can be planned more easily. However, when miles stretch across different states or even continents, logistics become more complex. Planning a visit involves considerations like fuel, airfare, accommodations, car rentals, and additional expenses, making every trip a well-thought-out journey.

Definition and Types of Long-Distance Relationships

Long-Distance Relationships (LDRs) encompass relationships between individuals who are physically separated for prolonged periods. These relationships require patience, maturity, and an understanding of the commitment involved. Technology has made it easier to maintain these connections, but various types of long-distance relationships exist based on duration and circumstances:

- **Short-Term Long-Distance Relationships:** Couples separated for just a few months.
- **LDBF (Long-Distance Best Friends):** Friends maintaining a connection through technology over long distances.
- **SVLD (Super Long Extreme Distance):** Extremely long-distance relationships, often spanning continents.
- **ECM (Early College Memory):** College friends maintaining their bond despite being in different locations.
- **LDK (Long Distance College Kids):** College students in romantic relationships dealing with distance.
- **IDS (International Distance Spouses):** Married couples committed to their relationship despite living in different countries.

As technology advances and global connections become more accessible, maintaining long-distance relationships has become easier. However, these relationships remain vulnerable to common issues faced by all couples, such as trust, loyalty, and third-party interference.

Common Challenges Faced in Long-Distance Relationships

Entering a long-distance relationship requires honest expectations and readiness for unexpected challenges. Not everyone is suited for long-distance dating, and the success rate varies among couples. Key considerations include the intended duration of separation and prior cohabitation. Discussing potential hurdles beforehand ensures alignment, but ultimately, the dedication and enthusiasm to make it work are invaluable.

One major challenge is maintaining effective communication. Long-distance relationships can strain the ability to interact efficiently, potentially shaping negative feelings into positive outcomes with conscious effort. The inherent nature and quality of individual partnerships play a significant role in determining the problems and difficulties faced.

Despite these challenges, with clear communication, mutual understanding, and commitment, long-distance relationships can thrive. Embracing the journey together and finding joy in the small moments can make the experience worthwhile.

CHAPTER 2

Communication Strategies

Effective communication is the backbone of any relationship, and it is even more vital in a long-distance relationship. Finding a communication method that suits both partners is essential. Virtual tools like video chats or messaging platforms help maintain the connection, but it's also important to schedule time for visits or meetings in person. Voice or video calls are particularly beneficial, as they convey tone and body language, which are crucial for human connection and understanding.

Text-based communication can sometimes lead to misunderstandings, making it necessary to establish clear communication expectations. Determine whether you will have regular video call dates or actively use messaging platforms. Both partners should feel heard and understood with whichever method is chosen. Digital reminders can help you stay in touch and schedule one-on-one time, such as virtual date nights.

Couples with large time zone differences can use a shared digital calendar to find a suitable time for both. If schedules don't align perfectly, digital "presents" can help maintain the connection. These could be simple like a photo or more elaborate, like planned emails with videos or notes attached. Handwritten notes shared digitally can also create a sense of human connection.

Effective Communication Tools and Platforms

In a long-distance relationship, communication methods vary from texts, phone calls, and video calls to even traditional snail mail. Numerous apps and networks available for instant messaging make it easy for you and your partner to choose the most convenient platform. As long as you're connected to the internet, you can make free voice or video calls.

Some popular communication tools include:

- **WhatsApp:** A versatile app that supports text, voice, and video calls.
- **Skype:** Ideal for video calls and excellent for long conversations.
- **Zoom:** Great for scheduled meetings or video calls with multiple participants.
- **Google Duo/Meet:** A user-friendly option for high-quality video calls.
- **Facetime:** Perfect for iPhone users, offering seamless video calls.
- **Email:** A thoughtful way to send longer messages or planned digital presents.

Besides choosing a suitable platform, you'll need to explore and utilize various communication tools and features. Messaging, sending winks, video and voice calls, and ensuring authenticity in profiles are some of the options available to make your communication more vibrant and engaging.

Setting Communication Expectations

Setting communication expectations is crucial in any relationship but becomes even more significant in a long-distance one. It's not just about the frequency of communication; it's also about defining the nature of communication during challenging times. Aligning on these expectations helps prevent misunderstandings, reduces anxiety and stress, and ensures that both partners feel validated.

Maintaining healthy communication involves recognizing that sometimes life happens—missed calls due to sleep, work schedules changes, or unforeseen events. Neither partner should feel guilty or stressed about these occurrences. Overcommunication can also become a burden, so it's essential to give each other space when needed, especially during stressful or challenging times.

Setting boundaries and modeling healthy communication patterns helps manage misunderstandings gently. If one partner feels overwhelmed, it's important to communicate this calmly and honestly. Remember, the goal is to foster a supportive and understanding relationship that can withstand the distance.

CHAPTER 3

Building Trust and Security

Building trust and security is fundamental to the vitality of any relationship. In a long-distance relationship, these elements become even more crucial. Trust is subjective and must be communicated and interpreted as a mutual respect for each other's individuality. It is essential that there is no underlying sense of insecurity and that both partners feel reassured of each other's love.

Creating security in a long-distance relationship involves a series of small, consistent behavioral patterns that foster trust. These patterns result in your partner's faith in you growing significantly, ensuring no hidden doubts and anticipating major relationship problems before they occur. When trust and security are established, you are free to live an independent, fulfilling, and exciting life, while maintaining a strong bond with your partner. Personal boundaries should be respected, and the need to ask for permission should not infringe on this independence. We will discuss ways to reassure your partner and avoid any doubt in detail.

Trust and security are sown in the initial phase of the relationship, if not before the couple parts. Research and surveys indicate that once the doubts and fears of the early stages are met and overcome, the resulting firm security surpasses the strength and dimension of any purely geographical bounds. It is tempting to cut short the phase of courtship to quickly establish mutual trust, but building trust takes time and deliberate effort.

Strategies for Building Trust in a Long-Distance Relationship

Intimacy plays a crucial role in reinforcing trust in a relationship. Staying as close as possible in the absence of a partner is essential. Intimacy should be strengthened by mutual respect and confidence that the partner will not take advantage of any vulnerabilities. Trust is built on the conviction that intimacy and secrets will remain secure.

Mutual respect and friendship lay the foundation for strong trust. Understanding that both partners' confidence in the relationship may waver at times is crucial. Building a positive impression and addressing insecurities through open communication and shared experiences can significantly strengthen the bond.

Strategies for building trust include:

- **Open Communication:** Regular, honest, and transparent communication helps build a strong foundation of trust.
- **Consistency:** Consistent behaviors and actions demonstrate reliability and dependability.
- **Support and Understanding:** Being supportive and understanding during challenging times fosters mutual confidence.
- **Shared Experiences:** Creating and sharing positive experiences, even virtually, helps strengthen the relationship.

These strategies create a secure foundation for a long-distance relationship, ensuring that trust grows and is maintained.

Dealing with Jealousy and Insecurities

Jealousy can cast dark shadows across any relationship, and it can occur even in the healthiest partnerships. In a long-distance relationship, it is normal to feel jealous from time to time. This is often rooted in low self-esteem and insecurities rather than a lack of trust. Addressing jealousy involves open communication and reassurance.

If you experience jealousy, it's important to talk it out and not let it fester. If you are on the receiving end of your partner's jealous emotions, offer comfort and reassurance. Show them that your relationship is built on positivity and love, not negativity and wrath. Reassure them frequently and demonstrate your commitment.

Insecurities can also creep into a long-distance relationship. You may feel like you're competing with your partner's surroundings or the people they are with. However, as long as both partners are committed to maintaining the relationship, there is no need to fret. Trust your partner and believe in the strength of your bond.

Handling insecurities involves:

- **Trusting Your Partner:** Believe in your partner's commitment to the relationship and avoid negative thoughts.
- **Open Communication:** Discuss insecurities openly and honestly to address any concerns.
- **Mutual Effort:** Both partners should make an effort to maintain the relationship and support each other.
- **Self-Confidence:** Build your own self-confidence and focus on the positive aspects of your relationship.

By addressing jealousy and insecurities, you can create a more stable and trusting relationship, ensuring that your long-distance love continues to thrive.

CHAPTER 4

Maintaining Intimacy

When physical closeness is not an option, emotional closeness becomes all the more critical. Living in different time zones can make face-to-face communication difficult and may lead to feelings of emotional isolation, which can magnify small issues into significant ones. Partners may lose sight of each other's feelings or needs, leading to disconnection as distractions cushion the emotional blow caused by communication gaps. Finding ways to bridge this gap and remain in sync can work wonders, showcasing your effort to stay connected despite the distance and strengthening your emotional and mental bond.

Discussing political, economic, and factual issues too often can become draining, and not being able to offer physical support can lead to emotional distress. Tending to your own needs can also become challenging, potentially aggravating dependency feelings that can sneak into long-distance relationships.

Physical closeness often determines the intimacy quotient in a relationship, so creativity is key in a long-distance one. Couples can explore various ways to keep the physical sparks alive, such as watching a film together while keeping a phone line open, reading poetry or favorite book passages, synchronizing bath times and sharing the experience, dressing up for each other, and exchanging weekly goodnight letters. These small gestures can create a fairy-tale sense of intimacy, reminiscent of childhood summer camps and the privilege of sharing your most intimate moments.

Cooking the same dinner for yourselves and each other can help maintain unity, adding a cozy and intimate touch to your meals. A new "kiss a day" rule—kissing a new part of your lover's body each time you are together—can keep the fire alive. Reliving moments by sharing the music you danced to can also strengthen the bond.

Creative Ways to Stay Connected and Intimate

There are countless creative ways to stay connected and maintain intimacy in a long-distance relationship:

1. **Watch Your Favorite Show Together:** Choose a show or movie to watch simultaneously, then share your thoughts and reactions throughout. Discuss the parts that made you laugh, cry, or cringe.
2. **Use a Period Tracking App Together:** With items syncing to the cloud or apps tracking your cycles, you can input key dates and track fertile days. It's intimate and practical, like syncing your breathing in a couple's yoga class.
3. **Send a Care Package with a Secret Note:** Include special items, like expensive lingerie, and a personal note. It adds a layer of intimacy and thoughtfulness.
4. **Schedule Time to Masturbate "Together":** Set a call to check in afterward. Try to climax simultaneously, creating a shared intimate experience.
5. **Send Flowers Just Because:** Surprise your partner with flowers without any specific occasion, or plan a surprise date. This can create delightful moments and lasting memories, making you feel closer even when apart.

The Role of Physical Intimacy in Long-Distance Relationships

Physical intimacy plays a significant role in any relationship, often underestimated when not discussed openly. In proximity relationships, physical gestures—whether verbal conversation, slight touches, or full-on embraces—serve as ways to express diverse emotions, reinforcing the human connection.

In long-distance relationships, physical intimacy takes on a different dimension. The anticipation and longing can intensify feelings, making the moments of physical connection even more cherished. Creativity and effort in maintaining physical intimacy become crucial.

Some ways to maintain physical intimacy include:

- **Virtual Physical Closeness:** Utilize video calls for face-to-face interaction, simulate physical presence by sharing activities, or using intimacy-enhancing devices.
- **Sensory Experiences:** Share sensory experiences by describing how things feel, taste, or smell during conversations.
- **Anticipation Building Activities:** Engage in activities that build anticipation for your next physical meeting, such as planning special dates or sharing intimate thoughts.

By embracing these strategies, couples can maintain a strong sense of intimacy despite the distance, ensuring that their relationship remains vibrant and fulfilling.

CHAPTER 5

Managing Time Zones and Schedules

Navigating scheduling in a long-distance relationship requires flexibility and creativity. Much of your communication may happen spontaneously, so it's important to make the most of the time you do have. Instead of seeing changing schedules as obstacles, embrace the one or two days a week you can consistently spend 15-30 minutes of quality time together.

Time zone differences add another layer of complexity. Ideally, you can have conversations when it's morning and evening for you, essentially having two calls that feel like one. The more aligned your time zones, the easier it will be to work around your schedules. For significant time differences, you might have to designate times for two separate hangs due to extensive breaks in between. It's not perfect, but it's better than nothing.

Once a week or on weekends, find a time that works for both of your schedules by scanning for windows of availability. If you have similar shifts, you might squeeze in a quick FaceTime before work or exchange messages during your mid-day break. Stay adaptable with these times, and if life gets in the way, reschedule without guilt. Substituting small or speedy interactions is better than calling out of the blue or surprise-visiting.

Here are some additional tips and tools to help manage time zones and schedules:

Tips for Managing Time Zones

1. **Use Time Zone Apps:** Apps like World Clock, Time Zone Converter, and Every Time Zone can help you easily track each other's time zones and find the best overlap for communication.
2. **Plan Ahead:** Create a weekly schedule and plan your calls or virtual dates in advance to ensure you have dedicated time for each other.
3. **Stay Flexible:** Understand that plans may change, and be willing to adapt your schedule as needed.
4. **Communicate Changes:** If your schedule changes, inform your partner as soon as possible to avoid miscommunication and ensure you can find an alternative time to connect.
5. **Share Calendars:** Use shared digital calendars like Google Calendar to keep track of each other's availability and set reminders for upcoming calls or virtual dates.

Tools for Scheduling

1. **Google Calendar:** Sync your schedules and set reminders for your calls or virtual dates.
2. **Doodle:** Use this scheduling tool to find the best time for both of you to connect, especially if you have varying schedules.
3. **Time Zone Converter:** Easily convert time zones and find suitable meeting times with this tool.

4. **Skype or Zoom:** Schedule regular video calls using these platforms, which offer built-in scheduling and reminders.
5. **WhatsApp:** Use this versatile app for quick messages, voice notes, or video calls. It also offers features like status updates to keep each other informed.

By leveraging these tips and tools, you can effectively manage your time zones and schedules, ensuring consistent and meaningful communication with your long-distance partner.

CHAPTER 6

Coping with Stress and Loneliness

Maintaining a long-distance relationship can be emotionally draining, leading to feelings of stress, loneliness, and emptiness. However, experiencing these emotions doesn't necessarily mean it's time to break it off. Instead, addressing and discussing these feelings with your partner can provide support and perspective, turning your relationship into a source of strength rather than additional stress.

Here are some strategies for coping with stress and loneliness in a long-distance relationship:

Communicate Openly About Your Feelings

Being open and honest about your emotions is essential. Share your feelings of stress and loneliness with your partner, and encourage them to do the same. This will help both of you understand each other better and provide mutual support. Discussing your emotions can also lead to finding solutions together, such as planning more regular virtual dates or finding new ways to stay connected.

Build a Support Network

Reaching out to other people who have been in or are currently maintaining long-distance relationships can be incredibly helpful.

Online communities, forums, and support groups can offer valuable advice and encouragement. Websites like the NetLetter provide resources for obtaining peer support, information on workshops, groups, surveys, and other helpful materials through its Online Support Voice Page. Additionally, the Coping with Loneliness and Stress Page from previous issues contains links to non-Net resources specializing in emotional well-being and healthy long-distance relationships.

Maintain a Balanced Lifestyle

It's essential to take care of your mental and physical health. Engage in regular exercise, eat healthily, and get enough sleep. Maintaining a balanced lifestyle can help reduce overall stress and improve your mood. Find hobbies and activities that you enjoy and that can serve as distractions from feelings of loneliness. Keeping yourself busy and engaged will make the distance feel more manageable.

Create a Routine

Establishing a routine can provide a sense of stability and predictability in your relationship. Plan regular check-ins, virtual dates, and activities that you can do together. Having a routine helps create a sense of normalcy and ensures that you and your partner stay connected. It also gives you both something to look forward to, which can help alleviate feelings of loneliness.

Focus on the Positive Aspects

While long-distance relationships come with their challenges, they also have unique benefits. Focus on the positive aspects, such as having more time for personal growth, developing strong communication skills, and building a deeper emotional connection. Remind yourself of the reasons why you're in this relationship and the future goals you share with your partner. Keeping a positive outlook can help you stay motivated and committed.

Seek Professional Help

If feelings of stress and loneliness become overwhelming, don't hesitate to seek professional help. A therapist or counselor can provide guidance and support tailored to your specific situation. They can help you develop coping strategies and offer a safe space to discuss your emotions. There are also online therapy options available, making it easier to access professional help regardless of your location.

Practice Self-Compassion

Be kind to yourself and recognize that it's okay to feel stressed and lonely at times. Practicing self-compassion involves acknowledging your emotions without judgment and treating yourself with the same kindness you would offer a friend. Take time for self-care activities that make you feel good and help you relax. Remember that you're doing your best to maintain a meaningful relationship despite the challenges.

By implementing these strategies, you can better cope with stress and loneliness, ensuring that your long-distance relationship remains fulfilling and resilient.

CHAPTER 7

Balancing Personal and Relationship Needs

In a successful long-distance relationship, both partners are attentive to their personal goals and need for independence, as well as the needs generated by their shared life. Healthy tension between these aspects can add spice to your relationship, making it more dynamic and exciting.

Balancing commitment to your work with your desire to be with your partner can be challenging. Conflicts often arise between educational or job-related aspirations and the impulses driving you to be with your partner. Here are some common conflicts:

- **Expression vs. Solitude:** One partner's need for expression may conflict with the other's need for solitude.
- **Financial Security vs. Presence:** The need for financial security may conflict with the desire to be with your partner, requiring last-minute flights and other logistical challenges.
- **Flirting and Dating vs. Intimacy:** One partner's need for heavy flirting and dating may conflict with the other's need for intimacy, snuggling, solitude, or intellectual conversations during their communication time.

To navigate these conflicts, consider the following strategies:

Prioritize Communication and Compromise

Open and honest communication is crucial. Discuss your personal goals and aspirations with your partner, and encourage them to do the same. Understand each other's needs and find ways to support them. Compromise is essential; find a balance that works for both of you without sacrificing your own aspirations.

Set Realistic Expectations

Be realistic about what you can achieve individually and as a couple. Set achievable goals and expectations, and be flexible when things don't go as planned. Acknowledge that both personal and relationship needs are important and that finding a balance may require adjustments along the way.

Plan and Coordinate

Plan and coordinate your schedules to ensure that you can dedicate time to both your personal and relationship needs. Use shared calendars and scheduling tools to find overlapping time for activities and communication. Regularly check in with each other to make sure you're staying on track with your goals.

Support Each Other's Growth

Encourage and support each other's personal growth and aspirations. Celebrate your partner's achievements and be there for them during challenging times. Remind each other that you're a team, working together towards a fulfilling and balanced life.

Maintain Individuality

While it's important to nurture your relationship, it's equally important to maintain your individuality. Pursue your interests, hobbies, and goals independently. This not only helps you grow as a person but also brings fresh energy and perspective to your relationship.

Create Shared Goals

In addition to your individual goals, create shared goals that you can work towards together. This could be planning future trips, setting relationship milestones, or working on a joint project. Shared goals help strengthen your bond and give you something to look forward to.

Practice Patience and Understanding

Balancing personal and relationship needs requires patience and understanding. Recognize that conflicts are a natural part of any relationship and that finding a balance is an ongoing process. Be patient with each other and remain committed to working through challenges together.

By implementing these strategies, you can find a healthy balance between your personal aspirations and relationship needs, ensuring that your long-distance relationship remains vibrant and fulfilling.

CHAPTER 8

Cultural and Interpersonal Differences in Long-Dis

Cultural and interpersonal differences can play a significant role in long-distance relationships, as they can lead to character development and personal growth. During your relationship, there is always a chance that both you and your partner will change or develop as individuals. These changes, influenced by cultural differences and evolving values, may lead to the discovery of new qualities in each other. While some of these qualities may be welcomed, others might be challenging to cope with, potentially causing tension.

Family, colleagues, and personal stressors contribute to these changes, making it difficult for your partner to understand who you are apart from the stresses and changes in your life. Regular life updates and sharing significant events can help you stay connected and support each other, even if you cannot personally relate to the challenges each other faces.

Strategies for Understanding and Managing Cultural Differences

Being ready and prepared to combat these barriers from the onset is crucial. Here are some strategies to help you navigate cultural and interpersonal differences in your long-distance relationship:

1. **Learn About Each Other's Cultures and Values:** Take the time to understand your partner's cultural background, values, and traditions. This will help you appreciate their perspective and reduce misunderstandings.
2. **Language Learning:** If your partner speaks a different language, consider learning some basic phrases or even taking language courses. This shows your commitment and makes communication more inclusive and meaningful.
3. **Regular Life Updates:** Share major events happening in your life and be there for each other during challenging times. Regular updates help maintain a strong emotional connection despite the distance.
4. **Open-Mindedness:** Leave biases and preconceived notions at the door. Approach your relationship with an open mind and a willingness to learn and grow together.
5. **Trust:** Build and maintain trust in your relationship. A lack of trust can lead to stress and negatively impact your relationship and health. Even minimal doubts can result in stress reactions.

Embracing Personal Growth and Differences

Recognize that personal growth is a natural part of any relationship. Here are some ways to embrace and manage personal growth and differences:

1. **Support Each Other's Development:** Encourage and support your partner's personal growth. Celebrate their achievements and be there for them during difficult times.
2. **Stay Connected:** Keep the lines of communication open. Share your thoughts, feelings, and experiences to maintain a deep emotional connection.
3. **Adaptability:** Be willing to adapt to changes in your relationship. Understand that both you and your partner may evolve over time, and flexibility is key to managing these changes.
4. **Create Shared Experiences:** Find ways to create shared experiences, even from a distance. Participate in activities that you both enjoy and that help you feel connected.
5. **Celebrate Diversity:** Embrace the diversity in your relationship. Celebrate the unique qualities and perspectives that each of you brings to the relationship.

By implementing these strategies and maintaining open communication, you can navigate the cultural and interpersonal differences in your long-distance relationship, ensuring a strong, healthy, and fulfilling connection.

CHAPTER 9

Support Systems and Community Resources

Developing a robust support system is crucial for any romantic relationship, but it holds even greater significance for long-distance ones. If you're hoping to marry or spend the rest of your life with your partner, finding ways to integrate them into your existing social group, or building a new one that suits both your needs and lifestyles, is essential. This network of support can provide emotional strength and stability, especially during challenging times.

Long-distance couples may also depend on community resources and support when dealing with stressors such as immigration, obtaining a co-sponsored green card, or managing the logistics of traveling back and forth to see each other. The more explicit you are with your support system about your needs, the better they can be there for you.

Creating a Supportive Network

If your immediate support system is a bit thin, don't fret. Not everyone has real-life people who "get it." However, in the modern age, long-distance couples can often find support and belonging online with the click of a button. Here are some ways to create a supportive network:

1. **Online Communities:** Join online forums, social media groups, and websites dedicated to long-distance relationships. These platforms provide a space to share experiences, seek advice, and find encouragement from others who understand your situation.
2. **Meetup Groups:** Search Meetup for groups that match your interests or lifestyle. Whether it's a long-distance relationship support group, a hobby-related group, or any other interest, connecting with like-minded individuals can be immensely supportive.
3. **Podcasts and Blogs:** Explore the growing world of long-distance relationship podcasts and blogs. These resources often share valuable insights, tips, and relatable stories, helping you feel less alone.
4. **Virtual Meetups:** Participate in virtual meetups organized by long-distance relationship communities. Engaging in these events can help you build connections and potentially make long-distance friends.
5. **Professional Support:** Consider seeking support from therapists or counselors who specialize in long-distance relationships. Professional guidance can provide tailored strategies and emotional support.

Leveraging Community Resources

Community resources can play a significant role in supporting long-distance couples. Here are some community resources to consider:

1. **Immigration Support:** Look for organizations that provide assistance with immigration processes, co-sponsored green

cards, and other related issues. These resources can help you navigate the complexities of immigration.
2. **Travel Resources:** Utilize travel agencies and online platforms that offer travel planning services, discounts, and advice. These resources can help you manage the logistics of frequent travel to see your partner.
3. **Local Support Groups:** Check if there are local support groups or organizations that offer resources for couples in long-distance relationships. These groups can provide emotional support and practical advice.
4. **Online Therapy:** Explore online therapy options that cater to long-distance relationships. Platforms like BetterHelp and Talkspace offer virtual counseling sessions, making professional support more accessible.

Widening Your Support Circle

There's always room for love and human connection. Widening your support circle involves:

1. **Incorporating Friends and Family:** Involve your friends and family in your relationship journey. Share your experiences and seek their support. Having a strong network of loved ones can make the distance more manageable.
2. **Making New Friends:** Be open to making new friends who understand your situation. Whether online or offline, building new friendships can provide additional support and companionship.
3. **Sharing Your Story:** Sharing your long-distance relationship story with others can inspire and connect you with people who may be going through similar experiences. It can also provide a sense of belonging and validation.

By developing a robust support system and leveraging community resources, you can ensure that your long-distance relationship remains strong, resilient, and fulfilling.

CHAPTER 10

Celebrating Milestones and Special Occasions

Even the smallest victories deserve celebration. Whether it's finding that perfect shirt, commemorating anniversaries, or marking personal achievements, each milestone is an opportunity to honor your relationship's journey. Celebrating these moments not only strengthens your bond but also highlights your commitment to keeping the relationship vibrant and resilient.

Creative Ideas for Celebrating Milestones

Here are some creative ideas to celebrate milestones and special occasions despite the distance:

1. **Virtual Watch Parties:** Use online services like Netflix Party, Zoom, Google Hangouts, Skype, or Shareplay. Watch a movie or binge-watch your favorite TV shows together, chatting about the best parts throughout.
2. **Game Nights:** Play collectible card games or online multiplayer games together. This can be a fun and interactive way to spend quality time and enjoy each other's company.
3. **Cook and Eat Together:** Plan a virtual cooking date. Choose a recipe, cook together while on a video call, and then enjoy

your meal at the same time. You can even theme your dishes based on different cultural cuisines.
4. **Virtual Travel:** Explore new destinations together through virtual tours and online travel experiences. Websites like Google Earth and YouTube offer a range of virtual tours, enabling you to travel the world from the comfort of your homes.
5. **Photo Albums:** Create a shared digital photo album where you can upload pictures from your daily life, past trips, and any special moments. This allows you to share visual memories and look back on them together.
6. **Personalized Gifts:** Send personalized gifts like engraved jewelry, custom-made photo books, or a framed picture that holds a special meaning in your relationship. These gifts add a personal touch and remind your partner how much you care.
7. **Shared Playlists:** Curate a playlist of songs that are meaningful to both of you. It could include tracks from your favorite artists, songs that remind you of each other, or tunes you both love to listen to together.
8. **Virtual Surprise Party:** Plan a virtual surprise party with friends and family. Coordinate with your partner's loved ones to join in on a video call and celebrate a special occasion together.

Marking the Calendar

Maintaining a calendar of special dates can help you stay aware of important milestones and plan celebrations in advance. Here are some tips for keeping track of these dates:

1. **Anniversaries:** Mark your relationship anniversaries, the day you first met, and other significant dates.

2. **Personal Achievements:** Celebrate personal achievements such as job promotions, academic accomplishments, and personal goals.
3. **Shared Goals:** Mark the dates for achieving shared goals or milestones in your relationship journey.
4. **Monthly Check-ins:** Plan monthly or bi-weekly check-ins where you can reflect on your relationship's progress and celebrate small victories.

Making It Special

The effort and thoughtfulness put into these celebrations make them special. Here are some additional tips to add that extra magic:

1. **Handwritten Letters:** Send handwritten letters or notes to your partner. Receiving a physical letter can feel incredibly personal and heartfelt.
2. **Video Messages:** Record a special video message for your partner that they can watch anytime they need a boost of love and encouragement.
3. **Surprise Deliveries:** Arrange for surprise deliveries like flowers, snacks, or a care package filled with their favorite items.
4. **Virtual Date Nights:** Plan virtual date nights with themes like a movie marathon, game night, or cooking class. Dress up as if you were going out, adding a touch of excitement to the occasion.
5. **Memory Jar:** Create a memory jar where you and your partner can write down special memories, inside jokes, or love notes. Share these memories during your video calls to relive cherished moments.

By implementing these creative ideas and thoughtful gestures, you can celebrate your milestones and special occasions in a way that keeps your long-distance relationship joyful and meaningful.

CHAPTER 11

Planning Visits and Reunions

Meeting in person is incredibly important in a long-distance relationship. Regular face-to-face contact helps maintain the connection and emotional intimacy. Early on in the relationship, discuss how often and consistently you plan to visit each other. Realistic expectations can prevent disappointment and keep the visits stress-free and enjoyable.

Collaborate on Planning

Plan visits together to ensure that both partners are equally involved. If one person always takes the lead, it can lead to feelings of imbalance or burden. Collaboration fosters a sense of teamwork and shared responsibility, making each visit more meaningful.

Tips for Collaborative Planning:

- **Discuss Frequency:** Decide on how often you can realistically visit each other, considering factors like distance, budget, and schedules.
- **Alternate Visits:** Take turns visiting each other to ensure both partners share the travel responsibilities.

- **Count Down Together:** Use countdown apps to track the days until your next reunion. This can help you both look forward to and prepare for the visit.
- **Remember Important Events:** Be aware of significant events in each other's lives, and plan visits around them to offer support and share in those moments.
- **Stay Flexible:** Understand that plans may change due to unforeseen circumstances. Be adaptable and reschedule without guilt when necessary.

Making Visits Special

To make each visit memorable, focus on creating special moments and shared experiences. Here are some ideas to enhance your reunions:

- **Explore New Places:** Discover new locations together, whether it's a new city, a hiking trail, or a cozy café. Shared adventures strengthen your bond.
- **Plan Date Nights:** Arrange special date nights with activities you both enjoy. This could be a fancy dinner, a movie night, or even a themed party at home.
- **Capture Memories:** Take photos and videos during your visits to create a visual record of your time together. These memories can help you feel connected when you're apart.
- **Celebrate Milestones:** Use your visits to celebrate personal and relationship milestones. Acknowledge achievements and special occasions with meaningful gestures.
- **Relax Together:** Sometimes, the best moments are the simplest. Spend quality time together relaxing, enjoying each other's company, and appreciating the presence of your partner.

Handle Reunions with Care

Reunions can be emotionally charged, so it's essential to handle them with care. Consider the following to make them smooth and enjoyable:

- **Manage Expectations:** Keep expectations realistic to avoid pressure or disappointment. Focus on enjoying the time together rather than achieving specific outcomes.
- **Communicate Openly:** Share your feelings and thoughts before, during, and after the visit. Discuss any concerns or anxieties to ensure you're both on the same page.
- **Stay Present:** Be fully present during your reunions. Limit distractions and devote your attention to your partner, making the most of every moment together.
- **Prepare for Goodbyes:** Saying goodbye can be tough. Plan something to look forward to after your reunion, like your next visit or a fun activity, to ease the transition.

By thoughtfully planning visits and reunions, you can strengthen your relationship, create lasting memories, and maintain a strong emotional connection despite the distance.

CHAPTER 12

Dealing with Transitions and Uncertainties

Relationships often go through various stages, and transitions can be particularly challenging. Moving from not long-distance to long-distance, from long-distance to living together, or even from long-distance to break-up are significant shifts that can feel nerve-wracking and terrifying. However, they also come with huge possibilities for growth and strengthening your bond.

These transitions will test your trust as a couple. It's natural to worry about what could go wrong amid the unknown, but the key is to handle these transitions proactively and positively.

Embracing Change and Transition

The best way to handle transitions is to move with the change, not against it. Embrace the new phase as an opportunity to strengthen your relationship. Here's how you can navigate various transitions:

Move-In Together:

- **Communication:** Discuss expectations, boundaries, and living arrangements ahead of time. Open communication can prevent misunderstandings.

- **Plan Together:** Collaborate on setting up your shared space and routines. This can make the transition smoother and more enjoyable.
- **Support:** Offer emotional support and patience as you both adjust to living together.

Going Long-Distance:

- **Set Expectations:** Clearly define how often you'll communicate and visit each other.
- **Stay Connected:** Use the communication strategies and creative ideas from previous sections to maintain your bond.
- **Trust and Reassurance:** Regularly reassure each other of your commitment and trust.

Breaking Up:

- **Honesty:** Be honest and clear about your feelings and reasons.
- **Support System:** Lean on your support system for emotional support during this difficult time.
- **Self-Care:** Focus on self-care and healing, allowing yourself time to process the transition.

Keeping the Trust Alive

Amid transitions, keeping the trust alive is fundamental. Here are some ways to reinforce trust:

- **Reassure Each Other:** Regularly reassure each other of your commitment and love. Trust is built on consistent actions and words.

- **Address Worries:** Talk about any concerns or anxieties openly. Addressing them early prevents misunderstandings and builds trust.
- **Celebrate Progress:** Recognize and celebrate the small victories and progress in your relationship. This reinforces positive feelings and trust.

Embracing New Hobbies and Activities

Taking up new hobbies or activities together can help mark the transition and strengthen your bond. Here are some ideas:

- **Virtual Classes:** Enroll in virtual classes together, such as cooking, painting, or language lessons.
- **Shared Projects:** Work on a shared project, like creating a photo album, writing a story, or designing something together.
- **Fitness Challenges:** Set fitness goals and motivate each other with virtual workouts or running challenges.
- **Exploring Interests:** Explore each other's interests by trying out new hobbies, like gardening, crafting, or learning a musical instrument.

Understanding and Accepting Change

Understanding that change is the only constant can help you navigate transitions smoothly. Here are some tips to embrace change:

- **Positive Mindset:** Approach transitions with a positive mindset, seeing them as opportunities for growth.
- **Patience:** Be patient with yourself and your partner as you both adapt to new circumstances.

- **Flexibility:** Stay flexible and open to adjusting your plans and expectations as needed.

By embracing transitions and uncertainties with a positive and proactive approach, you can strengthen your relationship and navigate the changes together.

CHAPTER 13

Self-Care and Personal Growth in Long-Distance Rel

For remote work professionals, engaging in self-care, setting personal goals, and trying out new hobbies are likely familiar concepts. These strategies are also crucial in maintaining long-distance relationships. Strength in any relationship, especially those separated by miles or oceans, starts with valuing self-care and personal growth. It's built on living positive, fulfilling lives outside of the time spent with our partners or loved ones.

Dr. Marcy Heath, Ph.D., emphasizes, "Viewing your time together as a 'bonus round' can enhance your overall life satisfaction and happiness, due to the personal time and effort you invest in your own hobbies, goals, self-care, and self-improvement."

The Importance of Self-Care

A great relationship might not always be the cheerleader boosting your confidence when you need it. That's why finding activities and practices that recharge and fulfill you is vital. Self-care involves doing things that make you feel good physically, emotionally, and mentally. Here are some self-care practices to consider:

1. **Exercise:** Regular physical activity can boost your mood and energy levels.
2. **Healthy Eating:** Nourish your body with healthy foods to feel your best.
3. **Mindfulness:** Practice mindfulness or meditation to reduce stress and stay grounded.
4. **Relaxation:** Take time to relax and unwind, whether it's through reading, taking a bath, or enjoying a hobby.
5. **Social Connections:** Maintain connections with friends and family to provide emotional support and reduce feelings of isolation.

Pursuing Personal Growth

Personal growth involves striving to achieve personal goals and investing in self-improvement. When you focus on your personal growth, you bring a fulfilled and enriched self to your relationship. Here are some ways to pursue personal growth:

1. **Set Goals:** Identify and set achievable personal goals, whether they are related to your career, education, or personal development.
2. **Learn New Skills:** Take up new hobbies or learn new skills that interest you. This could be anything from learning a new language to picking up a musical instrument.
3. **Read and Educate:** Read books, take online courses, or attend workshops to expand your knowledge and perspectives.
4. **Volunteer:** Engage in volunteer work or community service to give back and gain a sense of fulfillment.
5. **Reflect:** Take time to reflect on your experiences, learn from them, and plan for the future.

Embracing Solitude

It's important to embrace the solitude that comes with long-distance living. Use this time to focus on yourself and your passions. Here are some tips for embracing solitude:

1. **Enjoy "Me Time":** Dedicate time to activities that you enjoy and that help you relax and recharge.
2. **Self-Reflection:** Reflect on your thoughts and feelings to gain a deeper understanding of yourself.
3. **Creative Expression:** Engage in creative activities like writing, painting, or crafting to express yourself and find joy.
4. **Nature:** Spend time in nature to clear your mind and find peace.
5. **Gratitude:** Practice gratitude by acknowledging and appreciating the positive aspects of your life.

Communicating Personal Growth

Recognizing and communicating your personal development and milestones is essential in a long-distance relationship. Sharing your achievements and growth with your partner can strengthen your bond and give them another reason to love, admire, and respect you. Here are some ways to communicate personal growth:

1. **Share Updates:** Regularly update your partner on your personal goals, achievements, and experiences.
2. **Celebrate Milestones:** Celebrate your personal milestones together, even from a distance.
3. **Express Gratitude:** Show gratitude for your partner's support and their own personal growth.
4. **Encourage Each Other:** Encourage your partner in their personal growth journey and acknowledge their progress.

5. **Reflect Together:** Take time to reflect on your individual and shared growth as a couple.

By focusing on self-care and personal growth, you can maintain a healthy balance between your individual well-being and your relationship, ensuring that your long-distance love remains strong and fulfilling.

CHAPTER 14

The Future of Your Relationship: Setting Goals and

Securing a future together requires both partners to set clear goals and establish a direction for their relationship. When both of you share the same goal of being together, it simplifies long-term planning and reduces stress. Working towards a common goal fosters a sense of partnership and collaboration, making the relationship more robust and rewarding.

Setting Relationship Goals

Identify Common Goals: Discuss and identify shared goals for your future. This could include plans to live together, career aspirations, personal growth, or other significant life milestones. Knowing you're working together towards a common goal builds a sense of unity.

Create a Timeline: Develop a realistic timeline for achieving your shared goals. Outline the steps needed to reach these milestones and set achievable objectives along the way. This gives you both a clear path forward and something to look forward to.

Regular Check-ins: Schedule regular check-ins to discuss your progress and any adjustments needed. These conversations ensure you're both on the same page and can address any concerns or changes in your plans.

Celebrate Victories: Celebrate your achievements and milestones, no matter how small. Recognizing your progress keeps the relationship vibrant and alive, reinforcing your commitment to each other.

Managing Expectations

Open Communication: Be honest about your expectations, fears, and hopes. Open communication helps prevent misunderstandings and ensures both partners feel heard and understood.

Set Realistic Expectations: Establish realistic expectations about how often you'll see each other, how you'll handle conflicts, and what steps you'll take to achieve your goals. This helps manage disappointment and reduces stress.

Adaptability: Life is full of unexpected changes, so it's crucial to remain adaptable. Be willing to adjust your plans and goals as circumstances evolve, and support each other through these changes.

Evaluating the Relationship

Honest Assessments: Regularly evaluate the state of your relationship. This may require soul-searching and the courage to admit if the relationship isn't working. Avoid emotional antagonism and examine the situation critically.

Future Alignment: Ensure your lives are aligned in terms of goals and values. If both partners still share the dream of being together and have a clear vision for the future, continue working towards it. If not, it may be time to reassess the relationship's direction.

Plan for the Future: If you decide to continue the relationship, set future dating times and milestones to work towards. This creates a sense of purpose and direction, keeping the relationship focused and goal-oriented.

Scenario Planning

Consider Scenarios: Explore different scenarios for your future together. Discuss potential challenges and how you'll address them. This proactive approach helps you both feel prepared and reduces anxiety about the unknown.

Adjust Plans: Be willing to adjust your plans based on your discussions and evaluations. Flexibility is key to navigating the complexities of a long-distance relationship.

Visualize Success: Visualize your future together and the steps needed to achieve it. This positive outlook can help keep you motivated and committed to your shared goals.

By setting clear goals, managing expectations, and regularly evaluating your relationship, you can build a strong foundation for a successful and fulfilling future together. Long-distance relationships require effort, but with dedication and mutual support, you can create a beautiful and lasting bond.

CHAPTER 15

Case Studies and Success Stories

Sharing case studies and success stories can offer valuable insights and inspiration for those navigating long-distance relationships. These stories demonstrate the various paths couples have taken to maintain and strengthen their connections, providing hope and practical advice.

Case Study 1: Rebecca Washington-Crossley

Rebecca entered into a long-distance relationship in 2013/14, having previously dated people she worked with and, therefore, saw daily. The shortest distance she had ever been in a relationship over was 600 miles. She faced a new challenge with an 8-hour time difference. Maintaining spontaneity and keeping things fresh proved difficult. She said, "The difficulties with long-distance relationships, particularly with a time difference of 8 hours, is maintaining spontaneity and keeping things fresh. You talk so much over email and instant messenger, and you know all the big things happening in each other's lives, that it becomes easy to default to the same routine each time you meet."

Rebecca's experience led her to believe that varied communication types are essential to retaining excitement and strength in long-distance relationships. She found success by incorporating different methods and platforms to keep the connection dynamic.

Survey Findings:

- 59 survey respondents mentioned they started talking to their partner through **ILoveYourAccent**.
- Many successful responses came from the UK and the US, with a significant number of Americans reporting compatibility with partners residing in the UK.
- Five out of 13 American respondents had tried **YoungLove UK on Facebook**, which appeared to have a higher engagement rate among UK respondents.
- The findings highlight the importance of leveraging various social media and communication platforms to maintain and strengthen long-distance relationships.

Success Stories
Case Study 2: Mark and Anna
Mark and Anna met while traveling in Europe and soon found themselves in a long-distance relationship, with Mark living in the US and Anna in Poland. They maintained their relationship by planning regular visits, engaging in virtual date nights, and sharing hobbies such as online gaming and cooking together over video calls. After three years of long-distance, Anna moved to the US, and they are now happily married.

Case Study 3: Jamie and Sofia
Jamie and Sofia navigated a long-distance relationship between Australia and Canada. They prioritized open communication and trust, sending each other care packages and handwritten letters to keep the romance alive. They also took turns visiting each other and explored new places together during their visits. Their commitment

paid off, and after four years, Sofia moved to Australia, where they now live together and continue to grow their relationship.

Key Takeaways from Success Stories

1. **Varied Communication:** Incorporate different methods of communication to keep the relationship dynamic.
2. **Regular Visits:** Planning regular visits is crucial to maintaining the connection.
3. **Shared Activities:** Engage in activities that you can enjoy together, even from a distance.
4. **Support System:** Build a support network to help navigate the challenges of long-distance relationships.
5. **Celebrate Milestones:** Recognize and celebrate achievements and special moments to keep the relationship vibrant.
6. **Embrace Change:** Be adaptable and open to change as your relationship evolves.

These case studies and success stories highlight the importance of creativity, commitment, and support in maintaining successful long-distance relationships. By learning from these examples, you can find practical strategies and inspiration to strengthen your own relationship.

Conclusion and Final Tips

In conclusion, maintaining a long-distance relationship can be challenging, but with the right mindset and effort, it is entirely possible to see it through to the end. By maintaining healthy levels of communication and intimacy—be it through technology or traditional letters—and by having a realistic outlook on the future, you can preserve a strong connection. Enjoying each other's company while also living your own lives richly and fully will keep interests piqued and make you both happier in the long run.

Final Tips for Long-Distance Relationships

Here are some additional tips to help you navigate the challenges and thrive in your long-distance relationship:

1. **Keep Things in Perspective:** Remember that a few rough months or years apart will blend into the inevitable ups and downs of life. Focus on the bigger picture and the long-term goals you share with your partner.
2. **Plan Future Visits:** Always have another visit to look forward to. Whether it's a weekend visit next month or a holiday rendezvous several months away, keeping future plans exciting and clear can help maintain your bond.
3. **Learn New Skills:** Use your time apart to learn new skills and discover new interests. This keeps you interesting and intriguing to each other over the years, fostering personal growth and adding depth to your relationship.

4. **Take on Challenges:** Embrace challenges independently to show how you handle yourself and how you grow. This demonstrates resilience and adaptability, qualities that help strengthen your relationship.
5. **Stay Involved in Each Other's Lives:** Stay engaged in the aspects of each other's lives that matter most, such as family and old friends. Pay attention to your partner's experiences and share your own, fostering a deeper connection.

Remember, the key to a successful long-distance relationship lies in the commitment, effort, and love you both invest. By following the advice and strategies outlined in this guide, you can build a strong, fulfilling, and lasting relationship despite the miles apart.

Thank you for reading, and may your journey in long-distance love be filled with joy, growth, and endless possibilities.

www.ingramcontent.com/pod-product-compliance
Lightning Source LLC
LaVergne TN
LVHW092058060526
838201LV00047B/1451